Biff Helps After All

by Nat Gabriel

★

illustrated by
David McCall Johnston

Scott Foresman

Editorial Offices: Glenview, Illinois • New York, New York
Sales Offices: Reading, Massachusetts • Duluth, Georgia
Glenview, Illinois • Carrollton, Texas • Menlo Park, California

Today is the day!

What will we do?

Come on, Biff.

We will do something fun.

We will have a lot of fun.

We need something red.
What will it be?

That looks good.

We need something white.
What will it be?

That looks good.

That looks so good!

We need something blue.
What will it be?

That looks good.

But we need something more.

Dad helps.

Dad helps a lot.

Mom helps.

Mom helps a lot.

Biff does not help.

Run after him!

Catch him!

Run after him!
Catch him!

Look at my bike.

Come on, Biff.

Biff! Look!

That looks good after all!

Now we can laugh.